GW00400062

ALONE IN MY ROOM

□

KEN PICKERING

SOLO SCENES FOR YOUNG PERFORMERS

Dramatic Lines

DRAMATIC LINES, TWICKENHAM, ENGLAND
text copyright © Ken Pickering

This book is intended to provide resource material for speech and drama festivals, workshops, examinations and for use in schools and colleges. No permission is required for amateur performance.

Dramatic Lines
PO Box 201
Twickenham
TW2 5RQ
England

A CIP record for this book is available from the British Library

ISBN 0 9537770 0 6

Alone in My Room first published
in 2000
by
Dramatic Lines
Twickenham   England

Printed by The Dramatic Lines Press
Twickenham England

FOREWARD

On opening this book I found that that the anthologist was also the author or 'versioner' of most of the selected excerpts, a rare but useful occurrence. This allows Dr Pickering to speak with authority about the performance qualities of each text and give that 'out of the horse's mouth' advice, just a few economically chosen words, which instantly provide a pointer along the course.

In every selection from this collection the character is one which the performer may identify with in an attempt to come to terms with the traits and aspirations thrown up by the writing. These characters have lived through emotional situations that you may be able to relate to in your own life. Although the circumstances are different - those of Eagle Plume in America and William Harvey studying in Padua seem vastly removed - you will find that your life offers inner parallels with the characters and conflicts brought to your attention. What you have to do is recognise the similarities and develop the responses.

I hope you will thoroughly enjoy your acting and bring quality and light to your audience.

Paul Ransom

Chairman of The Society of Teachers of Speech and Drama

for
Paula, Lisa and Stephanie

INTRODUCTION

Acting a solo scene in a play, festival, examination or audition can be a frightening prospect but it can also provide some of the most wonderful moments of focus in drama. To be successful you must have a story to tell which fascinates, interests and excites your imagination. It may be a very personal story, an inner dialogue between parts of yourself, a current situation or something from long ago but it will engage an audience in a remarkable way if you take control of the material.

Firstly, you must know the scene so well that you feel you can do almost anything with it. This means being so confident of having memorised the words that you appear to be speaking spontaneously as a result of thoughts you are thinking. It is not only a question of knowing the lines but understanding precisely what is going on, how every aspect of your person - body, voice, eyes and facial expression will give vital clues to your audience. It means planning how you will use the available space and time, for only you can control these things, and it involves showing your audience the inner life of the character you are creating.

You will need to think how to dress for comfort, ease of movement and an indication of 'period'. You must portray the image of a person who knows how to present themselves for the work. You will need to show your scene to teachers, tutors or friends and be humble enough to realise that you will benefit from their comments; and you will discover many new possibilities in the scene as you progress.

Above all, you will only achieve good results if every detail of the scene is 'real' in your imagination and carefully shared with your audience. The acting notes are there to help but not confine you. Finally, you should know more about your scene than anyone else in the room and, in that sense, you are ideally alone.

These solo scenes are drawn from a wide variety of sources. The scenes specially created for this book are complete plays. The remainder are adaptations of scenes from plays, poems and novels and it would enrich any performance enormously if you read the complete work. However there is sufficient information contained within all the scenes for you to create magical moments of theatre, alone in your room and then, on stage.

Ken Pickering

CONTENTS

A YOUNG REFUGEE

A young refugee has been fleeing from the attack of hostile forces on the village. The whole family has fled but have become separated. Their route has taken them along the track of a railway line and the young refugee arrives dazed, tired and bewildered on the safe side of the border.

THE STAGE IS BARE.

THE REFUGEE: *ENTERS AND SPEAKS ALMOST IN A DREAM*

When I reached the border crossing they waved me straight through. Soldiers, rough men with hatred in their eyes. Standing there as if they couldn't care less about what is happening to us. I didn't dare stop or look back until I got here. I think I can stop now ..... but I can't look back.

STOPPING TO PUT DOWN A BUNDLE

This is all they let me bring. ..... My father was a teacher in the village but there's nothing left of the school now ..... I saw it in ruins the day before we came away ..... the day before **they** came.
"You've got ten minutes to get out"
said the leader,
"or we shoot the lot of you!"

SQUATTING DOWN

They had been shelling the village for days. Father said tanks were firing at us so at night we had to go down into the cellar. ..... That was at first ..... and then we had to stay in the cellar all day.
(PAUSE.) I saw ...... I saw ......

IT IS TOO PAINFUL TO CONTINUE

It took us four days to walk to the border. All the way down the railway track. There didn't seem to be any trains ..... just silence. ..... Then the sound of gunfire again and growing closer. We kept moving regardless, hundreds of us ..... somehow managed to keep going ..... on sips of water and a little bread snatched from home as we fled.

STANDING

I don't know where the rest of the family is ..... but I've got to find them. I don't understand how easily we became separated. We were all close together ...... then a few of us, the younger ones, ran on ahead. We heard the sound of aircraft overhead and scattered, diving into the woods beside the track. By the time the noise of the aircraft had died away it was dark. ...... Everyone crept out slowly, very afraid. There were bodies lying on the track ..... and I was totally alone ...... I couldn't find any of my family. *(WITH SIMPLE DESPAIR.)* They must be safe. They were always so careful.
(PAUSE.) And when it was daylight and I still couldn't find them, I thought that they must have overtaken me. ..... Everywhere, people looking for other people ..... everyone seemed to be lost ..... and we all had to keep going because we wouldn't be safe until we crossed the border.

MOVING AROUND CLUTCHING THE BUNDLE AND SHAKING HEAD

This world! It shouldn't be like this. No one in my family has ever done anyone any harm. Look at this place ...... mud, all mud. If it's like this now what will it be like in winter? How can I call this home? ......
I don't think the locals are too pleased either ..... too many of us. ..... I shall never forget the sight of the border crossing in the far distance with lines of people stretching as far as I could see ...... walking ..... driving cars ..... tractors ..... anything.

STANDING QUITE STILL

This is it, safety. ...... What's the use when you've lost everything? Why should we have to leave our home simply because there was some dispute over land hundreds of years ago ...... and someone insulted someone else because of a long held belief. We **can** live together ..... we've been doing it for years. Why has this happened?

STARTING WITH A JOLT

Oh! Gunfire, they're firing again ..... so near. They'll be bound to close the border if it's that close.

LOOKING BACK

Yes. They are closing it now.
(GASPING WITH REALISATION.) I said I wouldn't
look back ...... but I'm doing it!

PEERING HARD INTO THE DISTANCE

(PAUSE.) That's them! That's them! They've just
made it through. I'm sure that's my family coming
up the hill now.
(PAUSE.) They all look so exhausted ..... so ..... so sad.
And they think they've lost me.
(CALLING OUT.) I'm over here! I'm over here!
Where were you? Where have you been?

PUNCHING THE AIR WITH TRIUMPH

Yes! Yes! We've all made it!

ACTING NOTES

Sadly these events could have been taking place in many places during the last fifty
years. There is nothing sentimental about this speech: it is a fairly accurate version of
reality and you need to make it 'real' by trying to understand how a young person in this
situation would be feeling. Don't work too hard to put emotion 'into' the scene. The
simpler the approach, the better. The voice could almost be expressionless at times to
indicate that the character is emotionally drained and too tired and upset to show any
emotion. The body language should tell your audience that you have been walking for
four days: this will affect the pace of the scene which must be slow, yet varied enough
to show the depths of despair and heights of relief which all take place within a short
scene. If you see news coverage of refugees notice how they will often 'squat' rather
than sit in some circumstances.

The refugee may be played by a performer of either sex.

3

The Old Person Remembers and The Young Person Talks are taken from the play 'One Child at a Time', written to be performed by a teenage cast to help the work of Plan International which seeks to break the chain of poverty in the third world. The play is set in Thailand but could equally well take place in any of the 'developing' countries of the world where poor families living in rural areas are often forced to allow their children to go into the cities to find work and make money. They then lose touch with their children who are often exploited and used as cheap labour or involved in corrupt and criminal activity by unscrupulous adults.

THE OLD PERSON REMEMBERS

THE STAGE IS BARE AND WE ARE ASKED TO IMAGINE PEOPLE WORKING IN THE FIELDS.

THE OLD PERSON: *SQUATS DOWN ALONE AND SPEAKS DIRECTLY TO THE AUDIENCE*

The name of my country means 'land of the free'; but our children are sold into slavery. I remember a time when the village was alive with the sounds of children.
(*PAUSE AS IF REMEMBERING FONDLY.*) They played around the houses, hiding underneath them, running in and out. The school was full. (*SHORT PAUSE.*) The children did their assigned tasks so that we older people could carry on with our jobs. We cared for them and taught them skills so that, one day, they could look after themselves, and us in our old age.

STANDING SLOWLY

But where are they now? The village is quiet. I hear no laughter.

MOVING

The babies cry and their mothers weep for the brothers and sisters who have gone to the city. The headman of the village cannot help us. We meet, we take counsel, we discuss; but nothing can keep our children here.

LOOKING AROUND AND SPEAKING MORE URGENTLY

In our land, the family used to be the centre of our lives. It meant security ...... stability ..... respect. We were always taught that our collective well-being was all-important and each person must consider the consequences of our actions for others. *(PAUSING AS IF TOO UPSET TO GO ON.)* But now our families are destroyed. Our young are sacrificed to a distant god. We are doubly impoverished.

SQUATTING DOWN SLOWLY

Our poverty has robbed us of our dignity. There is no hope in the eyes of the people; only a craving for food and the absence of self-respect. *(LONG PAUSE.)* Our lives are barren.

WALKING OFF

EXIT.

ACTING NOTES

Enter the acting space very slowly and use this slow pace to squat and speak. Notice the marked pauses, but you will find others which will help create the idea of someone remembering. Be sure to let your voice fill the space even though the overall tone of the piece is quietly reflective. There is little physical movement but it is important that you focus very intently and any movements must be made in a very careful and controlled way. Give a great deal of thought to the position you will take up on the stage so that you can encompass an entire audience as you speak. Even though there will be a temptation to speak this almost as if the old person is thinking aloud, the intention of the speech is that it forms part of the narrative of the play, so address the audience directly.

The old person may be played by a performer of either sex.

from the play ONE CHILD AT A TIME by Ken Pickering
published by J. Garnet Miller Ltd
used with permission

THE YOUNG PERSON TALKS

The young person is living in the city. In earlier scenes the young person wore simple native costume but is now wearing modern 'western' clothing.

THE STAGE IS BARE.

YOUNG PERSON: *MOVES TO THE CENTRE OF THE STAGE TO TALK TO THE AUDIENCE*

I don't know what I'd say to my parents now. How could I tell them what I'm doing? They would be so hurt, they wouldn't be able to take it in.

LEANING AGAINST A WALL OR MOVING OFF

When I was at home in the village my mother used to say to me "Tai Ping, you are too young to be worrying about that." or "Tai Ping, you are too young to understand." She was always saying that! *(TENSING.)* Too young! These people don't think so. Here, children are fair game. As long as they get what they want, what do they care? They come in their flashy clothes, clicking their cameras. Tourists they call them ..... and we are part of the package!

ALMOST SPITTING WITH CONTEMPT AND SPEAKING MORE QUIETLY

My parents must be beside themselves. I wanted to write to them, but 'the syndicate' won't let us. I don't know what 'the syndicate' is exactly but that's what some of the older ones talk about. *(MISERABLY.)* 'The syndicate' controls our money, our time, our lives. Mother and father must think I've simply disappeared. Well, they're right, the child they know **has** disappeared. *(PAUSE.)* I don't think I could even talk to them now. They wouldn't recognise me. It's not just that I look different ...... I'm older. ...... Years older.

WALKING ABOUT DISTRACTEDLY

It's not even a generation gap. I've been where they have never been. I think we would be strangers if we met again.

(A CHANGE OF MOOD.) But I wonder what they are
doing now? I wonder where they are ...... at least
they've got a bit of money now ...... perhaps this can't
be all bad.
(SUDDENLY ANGRY AGAIN.) No, who am I kidding?
It's terrible ...... terrible for everyone ..... and I wish
I could see them again ..... I wish .....

HEARING A VOICE CALLING

Can't you leave me alone. This is hell ..... but there's no
way out now.
(CALLING.) Alright ...... I'm coming ....

RUNNING OFF

EXIT.

ACTING NOTES

There should be a restless and uncomfortable quality to this speech. The young
person has become 'street wise' and the body language should suggest somebody
who is defiant and rebellious. There should be plenty of variation in the vocal levels
here and an alternating sense of anger and sadness. Don't forget that this young
person has been suddenly robbed of his or her childhood: the disappearance of that
childhood, even though it was difficult, is deeply regretted. The adult world into which
the young person has entered is ruthless and the people are only interested in adult
pleasure and making money. Try to give the impression that this character has taken
a few precious moments to reveal real thoughts before being dragged back into
something of which to be ashamed. You may find it helpful to read the previous
speech which comes from the same play.

The young person may be played by a performer of either sex.

from the play ONE CHILD AT A TIME by Ken Pickering
published by J. Garnet Miller Ltd
used with permission

7

TURTLE ISLAND

Turtle Island was the name given to the earth in the creation stories of the Native Americans. In this play a tribe has gathered to consider a request made by the President of the United States to buy some 'Indian' land. The tribe responds by telling each other stories about the earth and their reply is based on a great speech made by Chief Seattle in 1854.

THE STAGE IS BARE

EAGLE-PLUME: *ADDRESSING THE GATHERING*

Are there no stories or visions that can give us hope?

LOOKING AROUND AND WAITING

We must consider the Great Chief's proposal before our brother, the sun takes his rest. How can we trust the white man to take care of our mother, the earth?

MOVING TO SPEAK TO EACH PART OF THE AUDIENCE WITH EACH QUESTION

The world as we know it is ending. We have no answer to the white man's guns. Where is the thicket? Gone! Where is the Eagle? Gone! And who is to say farewell to the swift pony? *(GRAVELY.)* The end of living and the beginning of survival.

COMING QUIETLY AND SLOWLY FORWARD

When the buffalo leave the plains it is a sign of things to come. There was war between the buffalo and the white men. The white men built forts and shot the buffalo as fast as they could. Up and down the plains came the hunters and after them the skinners. Sometimes there would be a pile of bones as high as a man stretching along the railroad track.

MOVING TO SPEAK TO ANOTHER PART OF THE AUDIENCE QUIETLY

The buffalo saw their day was over. Sadly the last remnant of the great herd gathered in council and decided what they could do.

SITTING AND THEN RISING

The Kiowa tribe were camped on one side of Mount Scott. One young woman got up very early in the morning. The dawn mist was still rising from Medicine Creek and, as she looked across the water, peering through the haze, she saw the last buffalo herd appear like a dream. Straight to Mount Scott the leader of the herd walked. As the young woman watched ......
(GESTURING.) ..... the face of the mountain opened.

CREATING THE IMPRESSION OF LOOKING INSIDE

Inside, the world was fresh and green as it had been when the young woman was a tiny child. The rivers ran clear, the wild plums were in blossom. Into this world of beauty the buffalo walked ......
(A LONG PAUSE.) ...... never to be seen again.

WALKING SLOWLY AWAY

EXIT.

ACTING NOTES

Dramatic story telling is one of the most important parts of acting: in one sense, you are always telling a story when you are acting. This is one of several speeches in this book which combine 'telling' and 'showing'. You can 'act out' some of the story as you tell it, the secret is to make the audience picture the action in their imaginations but you need to make sensible choices as to what you show. Imagine that a large tribe is gathered around you and that the audience is part of it. Use your concentration to focus your eyes: you might begin the piece sitting cross-legged and it may help you to look at old photographs of Native Americans and read some of their myths or listen to their chants as you prepare this speech. Take your time, there needs to be a feeling of wonder and mystery about this story, remember that you are describing an 'earth changing' event. Listen carefully to yourself and ask "Would I be moved by this story if I were listening?"

The native American may be played by a performer of either sex.

from the play TURTLE ISLAND by Ken Pickering and Philip Bass

9

ALONE IN MY ROOM

This speech is based on the opening moments of a musical 'Mothers and Daughters' which is about teenage daughters. In this scene, Lisa is alone in her room. She is a thoughtful and outgoing person who enjoys moments of privacy and she has a very vivid imagination.

THE STAGE REPRESENTS LISA'S BEDROOM. THERE IS A CHAIR AND A CD/CASSETTE PLAYER AND VARIOUS ITEMS OF CLOTHING STREWN AROUND. LISA IS TALKING TO HERSELF.

LISA: *CURLS UP ON THE FLOOR, IN A CHAIR OR LIES ON HER STOMACH*

Here in my room ...... I like to be alone. It's not that I'm unfriendly or there's anything I want to hide ...... it's just that I like to be by myself ...... on my own ...... posters on the wall ..... CD's and clothes all over the place. I have to mark out my territory.

LOOKING AROUND THE ROOM

I don't really call this untidy ..... I know where everything is and that's what matters ...... it's better, actually! I don't like people snooping around in here. ...... This business of having to come in here ...... and tidying up. ..... It's not fair. ..... I don't go barging into other people's rooms.

TURNING ON A TAPE OR CD

This is what they can't understand ...... my music. ...... Must have my music ...... then I can dream ...... 0 such dreams ....

SHE STARTS TO DANCE AROUND THE ROOM POSSIBLY PICKING UP A CUDDLY TOY

...... Yes, yes, yes. May I? ..... It's a pity I stopped going to dancing or I could be doing this on points!

SHE IS NOT QUITE SURE WHICH DANCE STYLE TO USE

Well actually I'm supposed to be doing my project.

FLOPPING DOWN AND SUDDENLY THOUGHTFUL

That's the trouble, really ..... I can't enjoy doing the
things I want to do because of the things I **have** to do.
(SIGHING.) This is totally boring ..... this project. I
have to ask all these questions and yet I'm not in the
least bit interested in the answers. I know that's a very
negative attitude ...... but how am I supposed to find
enough energy left to do music or dancing or drama
or just to enjoy myself when I've got all **this** to do?
(PAUSE.) I remember watching a programme where
the girl had a video camera in a cupboard and
she just popped in and spoke to it when she needed
to. That would be brilliant!

FACING AN IMAGINARY CAMERA

Dear Video-Diary. Hello. I just wish they would all
stop pressuring me and leave me alone. I wish they
would understand that this is **my** room and what **I** do
in here is nobody's business except mine. Today was
alright I suppose but I don't think I can get my project
done. ...... I think I'm suffering from repetitive stress
syndrome .....
(GASPING.) The only trouble is, they'd come and look
at the tape! Sorry, Video-Diary .....

SHE FINDS HER DIARY

..... I prefer the one I have with a small padlock on it.

*SHE OPENS IT CAREFULLY AND SMILES AS SHE
READS RE-LIVING SOME SMALL INCIDENT*

Stupid. Why did I do that? ..... He's mad.

SNAPPING THE DIARY CLOSED

I love this room, though. I don't want to leave it .....
ever. ..... Louise was only away for a short time ..... and
before she could get back her Mum and Dad had
sifted through all her personal stuff, taken everything
out of her room, boxed it up and **moved house** .....
without telling her! That would be **awful.** I don't know
how she coped. I'd go **mad.** I'd **hate** to move.

STANDING

The thing is ...... when I was about five I had all these imaginary friends ...... and they all lived in here with me. I used to snuggle down under the duvet and talk to them ..... and it was great because they always seemed to say what you wanted them to say ..... and some of them followed me around all the time. I can even remember their names ...... but I can't quite remember when I stopped talking to them. *(PAUSE.)* I don't think any of my real friends had friends like these. ...... Well, ... well, I don't **think** so ..... but I'd be too embarrassed to tell anyone ..... so perhaps they did.

SITTING

The point is ..... I think they're still here .... at least, not **'them'** exactly; but something like that. Watching over me, perhaps? *(PAUSE.)* I suppose it must be 'them' that I talk to all the time, though. ...... It's simply that 'they' change. *(PAUSE.)* **Well!** 'They' have now taken over a part of my brain ..... one side talks to the other now ..... we have these terrific arguments sometimes ..... not just inside my head but out loud ..... so I have to have somewhere to go ..... and not be disturbed. That's why I like my music so loud ...... so that nobody can hear me talking to myself ..... well, it's not actually **to** myself ..... it's more **with** myself. *(A LONG PAUSE.)* I wonder if anyone else does that? I don't think they do ..... all the other girls I know seem so normal, so .... so ..... confident. *(PAUSE.)* No. It's just me. That's why I need this room!

STANDING AND CALLING OUT

Shall I make a cuppa tea?

ACTING NOTES

Here is a situation that is probably very familiar to you: however much we enjoy other people's company, we also like to have our own 'space'. Try to recreate the sense of security and possible fantasy that 'the room' brings and establish it as small and your own by using a small acting area with defined boundaries and a few of your possessions strewn around. There are many mood changes in this piece and it explores how we find energy to do what we want to do very easily but often have to drive ourselves to do what we **have** to do! This is a conversation with yourself and the audience is eavesdropping on it. Use all the stage directions to help make that feeling of comfort and privacy with which the scene deals.

N.B. The performer should provide recorded music if possible (battery operated Cassette or CD player) to enhance the work.

This scene could be played by a boy with some adaptation.

adapted from the musical MOTHERS AND DAUGHTERS
by Ken Pickering and Keith Cole
available from Samuel French Ltd

THE CLASSROOM

This speech is very loosely based on Anton Chekhov's play The Cherry Orchard which includes a scene in which a family return to the house in which they grew up. Dee's younger brother has just started school and this provides Dee with the opportunity to revisit the classroom where he/she was in the reception class years previously.

THE STAGE IS ENTIRELY BARE EXCEPT FOR A CHAIR. THE ENVIRONMENT CAN BE CREATED IN THE IMAGINATION THROUGH THE DIALOGUE BUT IT IS A GOOD IDEA TO USE WHATEVER IS AVAILABLE. E.G. THE POSITION OF WINDOWS MIGHT INFLUENCE THE WAY THE SCENE IS PLAYED.

DEE: *ENTERS THE ROOM SLOWLY AND LOOKS AROUND*

(SNIFFING.) Well ...... still smells the same! but it's so **small** it used to seem much bigger than this. These tables are different ..... it's amazing to think we used to spend all day in here.

GOING OVER TO THE WINDOW

You can still see the Head's office from here ..... but the class teacher's luckier now ..... now the tree has grown so much bigger. When I was here the Head used to look across and stare straight in this window at our class teacher ..... poor Miss Gatman she must have felt we were always being watched.

THINKING BACK WITH AMUSEMENT

I remember those terrible twins from Vauxhall Road; they were **always** standing outside the Head's office. I was terrified of them and yet their Mum was quite kind ..... one of the dinner ladies ...... strange business.

MOVING TO THE CENTRE

Look at this! it looks like the same rug. ...... We used to sit around in a circle on this rug at the start of the day and talk about what we were going to do ..... and we'd all shout out at the same time. We used to make up stories and Miss Gatman would write them up on the board ..... and we'd copy out into

14

our books. We used to write diaries, too ..... like these
little books here. ..... Yeah! I remember that I spelt
canoe C.N.U. ..... I think we used to write down the first
thing that came into our heads.

LOOKING AT THE WALLS

Yes, **we** had these letters all round the wall, too .....
and we used to play a game recognising them. It's
incredible, when you think about it, you come
into this classroom for a year not knowing your N's
from your U's at the start and yet by the time you
leave you've started to read. ..... Well, most have .....
though there were several in my class who didn't.
...... It's strange ..... they didn't seem any different at first.
..... Makes you wonder what happens.

MOVING TO ONE SIDE

No! They've got a computer! Infants ..... with
computers! Well. Why not? Jo uses one at home,
so why not here? ...... The classroom door is kept shut
now, though. When I was here the door was always
open and we used to wander about all over the
school. You could go along that corridor to a place
where you could curl up quietly and read a book. ....
Sometimes our teacher would take us to a special
corner with a carpet and she'd read us stories. .....
I don't think they do that anymore.

LOOKING AT ANOTHER WALL

So, they've still got masterpieces on the wall ..... all
these paintings. ..... *(LAUGHING.)* Look at this!

*LOOKING AT A TABLE OF JARS, PALETTES AND
BRUSHES*

When we had painting we all wanted to be the one
who put out the jam jars of water.
(PAUSE.) I liked to mix all these colours together. I
used to think you could make wonderful colours if
you put them all together ...... but it always came out
brown.

MOVING TO THE CENTRE

15

..... Everything seems so low and small. I'm certain the room was bigger than this. I'd hate to be in here all day now. Look how low the ceiling is.

(PAUSE.) ..... I don't know how teachers keep a room so tidy. ..... We were always moving around the room and taking bits and pieces from one side to the other.

MOVING TO ONE SIDE

This is where I sat ..... and there was a girl called Sarah there ..... and Perkins ..... sat there.

(PAUSE.) Perkins was an odd boy. ...... I remember the supply teacher reading us a story about hedgehogs ..... and when he said, "And there was an army of hedgehogs," Perkins sniggered and drew a picture of these hedgehogs driving tanks and armoured personnel carriers! ..... That was typical of him.

(PAUSE.) At least, I **think** that teacher came here when we were in this class but it might have been the next year. ...... But I clearly remember he read us stories all the time ..... and wore a scruffy old jacket with round patches at the elbow.

AS IF TO LEAVE

Sometimes I wish I could be back here ..... go straight home from school and watch the box ..... the days were shorter then.

(PAUSE.) The school seems much older than it used to though. ..... I don't remember any mobile classrooms ..... I don't remember those. ..... There must be many more children now.

LEAVING THE ROOM WITH A LAST LOOK BACK

I don't really like change!

EXIT.

ACTING NOTES

Drama often deals with situations that are very close to us and here is a speech which explores something most of us have experienced. Before you start work on the scene talk to your teacher about re-visiting your old school or a part of your school where you used to go and try to establish the various feelings you had. It would probably be best to imagine that someone else is with you in this scene, but this person could easily be positioned where your audience is sitting. Don't be afraid to laugh at yourself as you remember the past and use a good area of the stage to represent the room. Move around with a sense of excitement once you have made the initial slow entrance. Be sure to have a clear picture of the room with all its contents in your mind as you perform, otherwise the acting will seem unconvincing and vague.

The young person may be played by a performer of either sex.

GULLIVER IN LILLIPUT

Gulliver has been shipwrecked and finds himself in the land of Lilliput where the people are only a few centimetres high. He is taken prisoner by a huge number of these tiny people but he is treated kindly and he also treats his captors with kindness. At the court of the Emperor he permits himself to be searched and allows some of the little people to go through his pockets. In this speech one of the young servants is trying to explain what they found on 'The Man Mountain'.

THE STAGE IS BARE. WE IMAGINE THE EMPEROR SITTING ON HIS THRONE WELL DOWN RIGHT OF THE SERVANT.

THE SERVANT: *BOWING LOW TO THE EMPEROR*

Your Majesty, in the right coat pocket of the great Man Mountain ..... after the strictest search ..... we found only one great piece of coarse cloth, large enough to be a carpet for your Majesty's chief room of state! In the left pocket, we saw a huge silver chest, with a cover of the same metal, which we were not able to lift. We asked him to open it and I stepped inside and found myself up to my knees in dust and ..... and ..... I've ..... been ..... ah ..... ah ..... sneezing ever since! Oh dear ..... I'm sorry, your Majesty.

TAKING OUT A HANDKERCHIEF AND BLOWING NOSE VERY LOUDLY

Just remembering it makes me ..... ah ..... ah ..... sneeze. In his right waistcoat pocket we found a prodigious bundle of white, thin substances, tied with a strong cable and marked with black figures ..... and we humbly think that this was writing: every figure almost half as large as the palms of our hands. In the left pocket there was a sort of ...... engine with about twenty long poles extending from it ..... rather like the palisade around your Majesty's palace. We rather think that the Man Mountain uses it to comb his hair but we didn't always trouble him with questions because we had great difficulty in making him understand us. In the right pocket of his 'middle cover' ..... your Majesty ..... we did not know what to call this item of clothing ..... but I think he called them 'breeches' ...... we found a hollow iron pillar about the length of a man, and this pillar was fastened to a strong piece of timber, larger than the pillar with strange figures cut into it and huge pieces of iron sticking out. ..... I do not know what to make of it, I'm afraid.

CONSULTING A WRITTEN LIST

Ah, now ..... in the smaller pocket on the right side ..... the Man Mountain has many pockets, your Majesty ..... there were several round, flat pieces of metal of different sizes, some white or even silver, some reddish and, and .....

HESITATING AS THE MEMORY BECOMES VERY VIVID

..... some of the silver pieces were so large and heavy that my comrade and I could hardly lift them.

REMEMBERING WITH EVEN MORE ANIMATION AS IF TELLING AN ADVENTURE STORY

In the left pocket were two black pillars, irregularly shaped but we couldn't reach the top when we stood in the bottom of the pocket and could only gaze up at them. One seemed to be all made in one part but at the top of the other there was a white, round substance about twice the size of our heads and there was a prodigious steel plate which we ordered him to show us because we thought these might be dangerous engines.

LAUGHING AT THEIR MISTAKE

He took them out of their cases and told us that, in his country, he used one of these to shave his beard and one to cut his meat! There were two pockets which we could not enter ..... and I think he called them his 'fobs'. They were like two slits cut into the top of his garment but squeezed very close by the pressure of his belly. Out of the right fob hung a great silver chain with a wonderful kind of engine at the bottom. We ordered him to draw out whatever was at the end of the chain and it appeared to be a globe, half made of silver and half of some mysterious transparent metal ..... ah ..... ah ...... (SNEEZING.). ..... No, it's true, your Majesty ...... it was transparent ..... and on the transparent side we saw strange figures drawn and we thought we could touch them but our fingers were stopped by that substance. He put this engine to our ears and it made a sound like a great water-mill ...... and we have come to the conclusion that it is either some unknown animal or it is the god that he worships. We rather think it is the latter because, if we understood him right, and it was difficult, he said he rarely did anything without consulting it and that it pointed out the time for every action of his life.

CONSULTING THE LIST AGAIN

Ah, yes. In the last pocket of all he took out a net big enough for a fisherman ...... and he could open and shut it like a purse ...... and inside there were several huge pieces of yellow metal ...... and if these were gold ...... they must be of immense value.

ADOPTING A VERY FORMAL MANNER

Your Majesty, having carried out your commands and searched all his pockets we did notice a belt around his waist made of the hide of some enormous animal and from this hung a sword about the length of five men ...... and on the right side of this belt was a pouch divided into chambers each capable of holding three of your Majesty's subjects ...... and in one of these cells or chambers were several globes of a most ponderous metal, about the size of our heads and in the other a heap of black grains.

SHRUGGING

I am afraid I have no idea of what these items were used for and the Man Mountain could not ...... or perhaps, would not, explain.

READING AGAIN VERY FORMALLY

This is the exact inventory of what we found around the body of the great Man Mountain, who treated us very kindly and respectfully.

BOWING AND LEAVING THE ROYAL PRESENCE
BACKWARDS

Your Majesty. ...... God save your Majesty.

ACTING NOTES

You can have a great deal of fun with this monologue and you might start working on it
by imagining how you would describe any familiar object if you were only a few
centimetres high. Never loose sight of the fact that Gulliver is twelve times the size of a
Lilliputian. In performance you need to recreate that sense of awe and wonderment that
the speaker obvious felt and can now remember. The servant often has difficulty
describing the objects in words alone and so uses body-language and gestures to help
in the description so it will be necessary to use your hands, face and indeed your whole
body to convey the ideas. Although the speaker is addressing an emperor, and must
therefore be very respectful, the enthusiasm and almost exaggerated awareness of the
hugeness of everything being described must keep the 'audience' fascinated. The
rather quaint language is very colourful and you should enjoy using it in a slightly
pompous and formal way. In performing this speech you will need to decide what
objects are being described. It will help you to know that they include: a snuff-box,
a small book, a comb, a pistol, a razor and a watch.

NB   You are strongly advised to read Chapter 2 of GULLIVER'S TRAVELS
       the eighteenth century satirical fable when preparing this speech.

The servant may be played by a performer of either sex.

GULLIVER IN LILLIPUT by Ken Pickering
a new dramatisation of Gulliver's Travels by Jonathan Swift

GULLIVER DEFEATS THE FLEET

Lilliput, the land of tiny people where Gulliver has landed, is at war with the neighbouring nation of Blefuscu which is also inhabited by tiny people and separated from Lilliput by a channel about 700 metres wide. The whole of the enemy fleet of ships is anchored in a harbour opposite the point where Gulliver is staying. Gulliver has offered to help the Emperor of Lilliput and has asked to be supplied with strong rope and metal bars to help him with his plan.

THE BARE STAGE REPRESENTS THE SHORE AND THE WATER. THERE ARE SEVERAL PROPS MENTIONED IN THIS SCENE BUT THEY CAN ALL BE 'MIMED'. GULLIVER IS LYING DOWN BEHIND A BUSH.

GULLIVER: *LOOKING ACROSS AT BLEFUSCU THROUGH A TELESCOPE*

I can see them clearly now ..... about fifty warships and ..... yes, those look like transport ships ..... all ready to sail when they get the next favourable wind. They obviously don't know about me so I had better try to stay hidden until the last possible moment. The Emperor's advisers told me that at the deepest point the water is about seventy glumgluffs deep ..... that's ..... about one and half metres ..... and the rest is only fifty glumgluffs ...... not much more than a metre ..... so I should be able to wade and swim without any problems. Now have I got everything I need? This thread isn't really thick enough, so if I twist it together, like this, it will be stronger.

HE BEGINS TO TWIST THE THREADS TOGETHER

They'll probably panic when they see me ...... I'd better not be too sure of myself ..... some of them will try firing their arrows at me. It'll sting a bit ..... but the only trouble is that I might get one in the eye.

HE STOPS AND THINKS

I know! glasses ..... my spectacles. They never did find them when they were searching me ..... perfect, if I wear them, my eyes will be protected.

LOOKING BACK AT WHAT HE IS DOING ONCE HE HAS FOUND HIS GLASSES

I need to twist these metal bars into hooks like this .....

HE DOES SO AND CONTINUES TO MAKE HOOKS AND TIE THEM TO THE ROPES

..... and then ...... if I tie one to the end of each rope. ..... That should do the trick! ..... If I pull the knot tightly ...... that's it! So ...... I need quite a few of these. ..... That should be enough.

STANDING

Blefuscu, here I come.

HE WALKS TOWARDS THE WATER'S EDGE

Oh! ...... it's cold. If I can bend down a little and then swim the deep part they may not see me coming. I must just make sure that my glasses are securely in place.

HE CONTINUES TO WADE AND TO SWIM THEN FINALLY STANDS SUDDENLY

I'm near enough now.
(SHOUTING.) Here I am, you people of Blefuscu, ... abandon your ships!
(LAUGHING.) I knew that would scare the life out of them. ..... Look at them all ..... jumping into the sea. ..... They're all swimming to the shore for safety. Now for the ships ..... if I can get one of these hooks attached to the bow of each ship I'll destroy them all.

HE STARTS WORK ON THE SHIPS BY ATTACHING A HOOK ON A ROPE TO EACH BOW

Ouch! ..... Ah! Arrows ..... they sting.

HE RUBS HIS ARMS AND FACE AS ARROWS ARE SHOT AT HIM BUT CONTINUES TO WORK HIS PLAN

Thank goodness my eyes are protected. I must get a hook onto every ship and I must **not** let go of these ropes. ..... Here's one I missed. .... These wretched arrows. ..... Stop shooting will you! Right, that's all of them. Now to pull the ships out to sea.

*HE MOVES AWAY AND HAULS ON THE ROPE TRYING
TO PULL THE ENTIRE FLEET OUT TO SEA. HE
STRUGGLES AND PULLS AGAIN AND AGAIN BUT
THE SHIPS WILL NOT MOVE*

This is ridiculous. They must move. ..... Why won't
they move?
(SUDDENLY REALISING.) Gulliver ..... you are so
stupid sometimes. Anchors ..... of course, they all have
anchors. I'll just have to cut through the cables. .....
Oh well! ..... it's back to the arrows.

*HE MOVES BACK WINCING AT THE ARROWS AND
PRODUCES A KNIFE FROM HIS POCKET*

This knife should cut these cables ..... yes ..... it does.
Wonderful ..... I'll soon have these ships floating freely.

HE CUTS THROUGH A GOOD NUMBER OF CABLES

And I must not let go of this rope or I'll have to start all
over again. ..... That's done it!. ..... All free. ..... Now to
haul them away.

*HE MOVES AWAY AND PULLS ON THE ROPE AND
FEELS THE ENTIRE FLEET START TO MOVE*

I've done it! The entire fleet in one great moment ......
if I move a bit faster I can get away from those arrows
...... and I hope there will be a hot bath and ointment
waiting for me.

*MOVING QUICKLY BACK TOWARDS THE SHORE
FROM WHICH HE CAME*

(SHOUTING.) Your Majesty. Your Majesty. The great
Man Mountain returns. Victory to Lilliput!

ACTING NOTES

The effectiveness of this scene depends largely on the accuracy of the physical action
which enables the audience to understand precisely what you are doing. Think very
carefully about the height, size and weight of the various objects described and work
especially on the sense of effort as you move through water, pull on ropes or wince as

24

you feel the arrows stinging your flesh. It is worth taking great trouble over the 'props' for this scene and arranging the imagined strip of sea at a point which will enable all your facial expressions to be seen as you approach the other side. Try to think yourself into being a giant as you begin the scene and be sure to think what kind of glasses would be worn by a person in the eighteenth century.

NB   You are strongly advised to read Chapter 5 of GULLIVER'S TRAVELS
        the eighteenth century satirical fable when preparing this speech.

GULLIVER IN LILLIPUT by Ken Pickering
a new dramatisation of Gulliver's Travels by Jonathan Swift

NETOCHKA NEZVANOVA

Netochka Nezvanova is an unfinished story set in the late nineteenth-century and written by the great Russian author Dostoyevsky. Netochka is a young girl who has been abandoned by her father who treated her cruelly and her mother who was unable to cope with the situation. She has been found unconscious in the streets of the fashionable city of St. Petersburg and taken in by an aristocratic family. Although they are very kind to her at first she is increasingly uncomfortable with the behaviour of the young Princess Katya with whom she is desperate to make friends. In this scene, Netochka is now well enough to be out of bed but is alone.

THE STAGE REPRESENTS A HUGE BEAUTIFULLY FURNISHED ROOM.

NETOCHKA: *SEATED ON A CHAIR*

Oh. I wish Katya would be more friendly ..... I really want her to like me ..... but I never know what to do when she is here. Sometimes she is very kind ..... and other times ...... I don't know.

SINKING BACK ON THE CHAIR

The other day she came to me when I was still in bed ..... I was still too weak to be up all day ..... and she said, "Well? Do you like me coming to talk to you?"
Well, **of course** I do, so I said,
"Yes, I do very much. Come more often."
So she said,
"They told me it would cheer you up if I came to see you, but do hurry and get well."
..... She seemed so impatient, and she speaks in a rather abrupt way.
(PAUSING.) And then ..... she suddenly looked at me and said,
(SHE IMITATES THE CLIPPED SPEECH OF KATYA.)
"Why are you always so quiet?"
I didn't really know what to say; so I said,
"I just am."
And then our conversation went like this: She said,
"I suppose you're always thinking."
..... "Yes, I think a lot."
"They tell me that I talk too much and think too little. Is it really so bad to be talkative?"
...... "No, I like it when you talk."
"Hmmm ..... but what do you think about?"

26

STANDING

I was rather embarrassed by this question because
I have to admit that I think about her a lot ..... so I
eventually plucked up courage and said,
"I think about you."
And she said,
"Does it make you happy?"
(PAUSE AS IF ANSWERING.) "Well, yes!"

ACTING OUT THE REMEMBERED DIALOGUE

"Then that means you must like me?"
"Yes!"
"Well, I don't like you yet. You're so thin. I'm going to
bring you that cake I promised later on. Well, goodbye
for now."
And then she kissed me and ran out of the room. But
after dinner the cake really did arrive. She ran in ..... all
giggling and frenzied because she had brought
something and she said,
"Eat it all ..... eat more, eat more, it's my cake. ..... Well,
goodbye!"
And that was all I saw of her.

LOOKING AROUND RATHER WISTFULLY

There was another time when she suddenly came
flying in to see me at an unusual time ..... her black
curly hair was wild and her cheeks looked as if they
were on fire ..... and her eyes were sparkling .....
(REMEMBERING ALMOST BREATHLESSLY.)
..... and she shouted out,
"Can you play badminton?"
I was so miserable that I could not say
"Yes."
but I just had to say
..... "No."
And she replied,
"What a funny thing you are. Well, hurry up and get
better, then I'll teach you. I only came to find out.
Now I'm going to play with Madame Leotard.
Goodbye, they're waiting for me."
That's just like her ..... I never quite know where I am
with her. I do like her **so** much but I don't know
if she likes me yet.

SITTING

Now that I am allowed to be up all day I ought to be able to spend a lot of time with Katya. ..... She's not like anyone I've ever known before, she always seems so confident and she doesn't seem to mind what she says to anyone. I wish I could be like that.

SITTING ALERT ON THE EDGE OF THE CHAIR

The other day, when we had been playing a game together, I got very excited and I threw my arms around her neck and kissed her ..... just like she does to me sometimes; ..... and she grabbed me by the hand and frowned at me as if I had offended her terribly ......
(REMEMBERING PAINFULLY.) ...... and she asked me "What are you doing? Why are you kissing me?" And I was so embarrassed, as though I had done something terribly wrong. I was so startled by her abrupt question I didn't answer ..... and she just shrugged her shoulders and sat down in the corner of the sofa ......
(IMITATING WHAT SHE REMEMBERS.) ..... with her lips all puffy ..... and just **stared** at me for a long time. ..... Like this. ..... I wanted to cry and I could feel the tears coming but I was determined that she would not see me cry ..... because I know what she would have said.
(IN A CLIPPED VOICE.) "Why are you crying?"
(PAUSE.) I sometimes wish I was back with my father ...... but then ....
(PAUSE.) When I was very young I used to look across the street at a house like this and long to see what was going on behind those grand curtains ..... I suppose I know now.

LEAVING RATHER SLOWLY AND SADLY

EXIT.

ACTING NOTES

A long skirt or dress and suitable footwear are essential for this scene. Netochka is still weak but don't forget that this story is set in a time when people were probably more likely to express fondness for each other than we are! You need to create a vivid picture of this other girl who is such a mystery and fascination to you. Try to convey the effect of your bewilderment and sadness together with your anxiety to please. There does not need to be a great deal of expansive movement here but your body must show tension and excitement.

adapted from the novel NETOCHKA NEZVANOVA by Fyodor Dostoyevsky
available in translation in the Penguin Classics series

MRS BLAKE'S PRIZE

Sam is a bright and enthusiastic young student who is trying to earn some extra money by working as a Telesales person.

SAM SITS CENTRE STAGE AT A TABLE WITH A TELEPHONE.

SAM: *DIALLING*

Mrs Blake ?
(SHORT PAUSE FOR MRS BLAKE ....)
I've got some really good news for you, Mrs Blake. This is Sam from Leisure Seekers International Mrs Blake and our computer has just been selecting the winners of our wonderful Sunlover competition and it's come up with your name! Congratulations Mrs Blake!
(MRS BLAKE ....)
That's alright Mrs Blake, you may not realise you had entered but the computer has simply come up with your name. It's your lucky day!
(MRS BLAKE ....)
It's terrific news, Mrs Blake ..... you have certainly won for yourself a free holiday in the sun.

INCREASINGLY AWARE THAT MRS BLAKE IS BAFFLED AND NOT TOO INTERESTED

And your name has also been entered into our competition to win a brand new Peugeot car **and** you will have one of our Elizabethan hostess sets.

MRS BLAKE IS OBVIOUSLY NOW A LITTLE MORE INTERESTED AND SAYS SHE WILL TELL HER HUSBAND

All we ask, Mrs Blake, is that you and Mr Blake come to our special presentation in London next Thursday to claim your prize.
(MRS BLAKE ....)
I'm sorry Mrs Blake, there's a lot of noise going on here. I didn't quite hear what you said.
(MRS BLAKE ....)
It last about an hour.

MRS BLAKE'S QUESTIONS AND DOUBTS ARE
BECOMING TIRESOME

We'll tell you about the holiday you have won in one
of our fabulous resorts.
(MRS BLAKE ....)
No, I'm afraid I can't tell you now. We like to speak to
couples in person.
(MRS BLAKE....)
Oh. I'm sure your husband **will** want to come when
he hears that you have both won a dream holiday.
..... **I** would.
(LAUGHING WITH RATHER FORCED HUMOUR.)
Oh. We'll soon change that, won't we, Mrs Blake!
(MRS BLAKE....)
There will be other winners too, of course, ... but .....
you've won the **top** prize.
Now would you like to come at seven o'clock or
eight?
(MRS BLAKE ....)
Oh, don't worry about them. You can leave all the
arrangements to us, Mrs Blake.
(MRS BLAKE.....)
Yes ..... about an hour.

DROPPING THE POLITE VOICE AND CALLING TO
SOMEONE ELSE

Cor ..... I've got a tricky one 'ere!
(LISTENING TO MRS BLAKE WITH DISINTEREST.)
I **am** still here, Mrs Blake.
(MRS BLAKE .....)
Forty-eight Jermin Street, just off Oxford Street. You
can't miss it, it's the head office of Leisure Seekers
International. ..... We'll look forward to seeing you .....
just give your name at reception ..... and they'll tell you
where to go.
(MRS BLAKE ....)
I'm sure you look smart all the time Mrs Blake. Come
as you feel comfortable.

SAM IS GROWING INCREASINGLY FRUSTRATED

The presentation? Well, we do Mrs Blake ..... you
see our presentation is a special event for our
winners. ...... You just go round it and watch.

*IT'S OBVIOUS THAT MRS BLAKE HAS UNDERSTOOD
THE WORD PRESENTATION TO MEAN SOMETHING
ENTIRELY DIFFERENT*

You'll enjoy it Mrs Blake ..... especially the video.
(MRS BLAKE ....)
Yes ..... you've certainly won, Mrs Blake. ..... You won't
be disappointed ..... all we ask is that you give us an
hour of your time

*MRS BLAKE CAN'T UNDERSTAND WHY IT TAKES AN
HOUR TO GIVE HER THE PRIZE AND SHE'S QUITE
SURE MR BLAKE WON'T BE IMPRESSED*

Real stop at home, he is. Is he? Well, we all know
what these men are like. Don't we, Mrs Blake?
(MRS BLAKE ....)
Well, I have to work in the evenings ..... we have to be
available for our customers at all times.
(MRS BLAKE ....)
Yes. I do have a home to go to ......
(MRS BLAKE ....)
We are a major international company.
(MRS BLAKE ....)
Mrs Blake ..... there are many aspects to our
business. .....
(MRS BLAKE ....)
When you are with us you can be sure you are
in safe hands.

SAM IS DESPERATE TO GET OFF THE 'PHONE NOW

All the noise you can hear? This is a very busy office
Mrs Blake.
(MRS BLAKE ....)
Yes ..... even at this time of night. Busy bees here,
Mrs Blake.

*TRYING VERY HARD TO REMAIN PLEASANT AND
CHEERFUL*

No, our computers just came up with the names of
the winners and you were one of them.
(MRS BLAKE ....)
How did it get in there?
(MRS BLAKE ....)

It's funny isn't it. I mean ..... I don't understand
computers either, really.

RELIEVED

Now, that I **can** tell you. It's in Palais des Ingles .....
in the Algarve.
(MRS BLAKE ....)
No, Mrs. Blake. Where've you been?
(MRS BLAKE ....)
Portugal ..... it's Portugal ..... and ever so nice over
there. It's a really beautiful development. You know,
own swimming pool, lawns, balcony with a
view ...... entertainment in the evenings. ...... It's lovely,
..... air conditioning in all the rooms, en suite bath,
and so on.

MRS BLAKE THINKS IT SOUNDS DREADFUL

Oh! Mrs Blake, how can you say that? Give yourself
a break, you deserve it, spoil yourself. This is the
opportunity of a lifetime. Think of Mr Blake.
(MRS BLAKE ....)
No. I'm very sorry ..... that's a bit difficult. I can't really
hold it like that. You see we may have to offer your
prize to the next person if you don't want to take it up.
(MRS BLAKE ....)
Oh. It certainly did! There's no doubt about that,
it **did** select you first .....
(MRS BLAKE ....)
.... but there were other names.
(MRS BLAKE ....)
Well ..... quite a few ..... but **yours** was there at the top.
I can assure you of that.
(MRS BLAKE ....)
No. I suppose not, Mrs Blake. Could you ring me back
in ten minutes?
(MRS BLAKE ....)
No. I'm afraid that won't be possible. ..... I won't be
here tomorrow.

PUTS THE PHONE DOWN EXHAUSTED

ACTING NOTES

Although Sam is confined to the telephone throughout this scene the drama comes from the responses and the growing sense of frustration with the call. Sam has learned the 'sales patter' very well but is not prepared for all the questions. You will need to imagine that the room is full of 'telesales' people all desperately trying to do the job and realise that Sam may have difficulty in hearing Mrs Blake to add to the problems. As you work on the speech you will need to construct imaginary responses to your remarks. It's a good idea to start with an improvised rehearsal of the idea before getting down to the actual text. Sam has a special 'telephone' voice which might disappear under pressure and is not there when chatting to friends. The audience must 'read' much of what is happening in your facial expression. You should be able to create a very funny scene.

Sam may be played by a performer of either sex.

AN ORDEAL

Kim is waiting to go into a drama or dance examination.

THE STAGE IS BARE EXCEPT FOR A CHAIR.

KIM: *SEATED TENSELY HOLDING A FEW PAPERS*

I am **so** nervous! I always am. I can feel my
stomach churning over and over.

INDIGNANTLY ADDRESSING STOMACH

Stop churning, will you! How much longer is she
going to be in there? What are they doing?
(PAUSE.) I can't hear anything. Perhaps they've
gone to sleep! My teacher has told me that there
was an exam where the examiner went to sleep,
honestly, there was. She wondered where her little
pupil had gone and after a **very** long time plucked
up courage and tapped on the door but there was
no answer ..... and so she opened the door very
slowly ..... and there was the little girl standing in the
middle of the room in front of the table ..... and the
examiner was fast asleep ..... just nodded off! It's true,
honestly. Apparently it was the end of a very long
day and the examiner had been travelling around all
over the place.
(PAUSING TO STRETCH.) I wish I didn't get so
nervous. My sister doesn't ...... or if she does she
doesn't show it. She just sails in and when she
comes out and you ask how it went she says, "OK"
...... and that's it! She's always OK.

*SHRUGGING AND THEN REMEMBERING WHAT IS
COMING*

I bet I forget how it goes. I've gone over and over
the whole thing in my mind but sometimes I just go
blank. Don't know why ..... it just happens ..... without
any warning. And you feel so stupid.
(PAUSE.) I know it. I know it. I know. I know it!
(CONTINUING TO SPEAK SEVERELY TO SELF.)
If you forget it this time I'm never doing this again.
(PAUSING.) I did read ....
(THINKING HARD.) ..... about this famous actor, Irving
..... Sir Henry Irving. ..... Well, he was the first actor

35

ever to be knighted ..... but when he first appeared on
stage he walked on and just stood there because
he'd forgotten his lines, so he ran off again. Can you
imagine? Just ran out!
(PAUSE.) If I forgot what I was supposed to do in
there ..... and I ran out ..... imagine what my teacher
would say! "Just you go back in there and try again!"
(SNIGGERING.) I suppose I ought to be grateful to
old Irving. If he could do it! .....

STANDING

..... I ..... I really ought to be warming up.

*STRETCHING A FEW TIMES OR TAKING A FEW DEEP
BREATHS*

Funny, there doesn't seem to be anyone around.
I hope today's the right day.

BRIGHTENING

Perhaps I've missed it. Perhaps my exam was
yesterday!

LOOKING AT THE PAPERS

No. It's today. That's today's date. .....
(SIGHING) You never quite know how they are going
to look at you. Sometimes they smile ...... but you
can't really tell what they're thinking. Sometimes they
look dead bored. Some of them seem to be able to
do everything at once. ..... This friend of mine went
into a drama exam and when she came out she said
"That examiner didn't look at me once ..... didn't watch
at all!" And then, when she got the report it said 'You
should have used your left hand!' You see the
examiner'd been watching all the time.
(THOUGHTFULLY.) In some ways I prefer festivals .....
'cos the adjudicator's miles away down a huge hall.
You can't see what expression they have on their
faces from that distance. Those festivals are mad!
Hundreds and hundreds of parents clucking around
and everyone getting hysterical ..... but at least you
have a proper audience.
(PAUSE.) Some of them go on for weeks. .....
I almost feel sorry for the adjudicators

imagine having to see the same old stuff over and over again. How **do** they keep sane?

CURLING UP ON THE CHAIR AGAIN

I wonder how some of them got there. ..... I mean ...... why are they there and me here? How do you **become** one of them? Examiner or adjudicator? Which? Why? ..... and ..... What have **they** done? *(PAUSE.)* I think it's a man this time ..... last time it was a woman ...... doesn't worry me particularly either way because I try my hardest to pretend they aren't there anyway! Jo said "There's no need to be nervous." It's all right for her ..... she never does this crazy thing.
(PAUSE TO THINK.) Perhaps it's not entirely crazy because if you can do this you ought to be able to do a lot of things ..... and I do enjoy it in a way. It's ..... it's ..... satisfying, I suppose. ..... **If** you can remember, that is. That's the problem, remembering. I'm sure that most other people don't have my problem.
I simply can't remember what comes next ..... or even what comes first.

AWARE OF MOVEMENT OUTSIDE

Oh! It's me.

STANDING IN RESIGNED MANNER

It's me!

MOVING OFF

EXIT.

ACTING NOTES

Here is your chance to take a gently ironic look at the world of examinations, festivals and auditions! Work to build the tension of waiting by never sitting or standing comfortably. Try to develop a nervous laugh or a sense of almost false jollity as you try to develop some courage. This is really an 'inner dialogue' between various parts of yourself but be absolutely clear about where the actual examination is taking place so that your 'audience' can feel the focus of your anxiety. There are good opportunities for some graphic story-telling here. Give plenty of attack.

I WANTED TO DANCE

In this speech Alison explains that her great disappointment is that she was never allowed to go to dancing classes, whereas her sister, Sarah goes to dancing classes several evenings a week.

THERE IS A BARE STAGE WITH A CHAIR DOWN RIGHT OF CENTRE.

ALISON: *MOVING RATHER DREAMILY AROUND THE ROOM*

I always wanted to be a dancer.
(PAUSE.) Well, I always wanted to go to dancing classes ..... but my mum said I'd 'grown too big'. That's ridiculous! ..... Should you have to be a certain size to be allowed to dance? ..... Everybody should dance ..... at least, I think they should.

SITS

She let Sarah go ...... let my sister. She said Sarah was 'petite', so that was OK.
(WITH SOME CONTEMPT.) 'Petite' indeed! So now she does it **all!** ..... ballet ..... tap ..... modern ..... jazz ..... even Spanish now. She's there nearly every night **and** Saturday morning.
(PAUSE.) When she was very little and she'd just started I even had to take her.
(REMEMBERING.) I really envied those girls ..... so slim in their leotards ..... and the way they behaved towards 'Madame' as she's called. ..... Not that I would mind being called Madame, actually.
(PAUSE.) They're all the same, dancers, give themselves fancy names ...... and the old ones always gave themselves Russian names. ..... I don't really know why! What was the point of that? ..... There's nothing wrong with my own name. And I'm proud of it.

STANDING AND MOVING

I suppose it's the magic I wanted. When you see dancers gliding in as if they don't weigh anything at all, *(SIGHING.)* it looks so romantic. Although I know it's agony for them most of the time! but it must be wonderful to feel the music just .... carry you along.
(LAUGHING TO HERSELF.)

I don't think it's really quite like that at Sarah's classes
though ..... the lady playing the piano just plonks
along .....

IMITATING

..... like an automaton.
(PAUSE.) When I was **very** small my mum and dad
had a vinyl record of 'Swan Lake' ..... it was very old
and scratchy even then ..... but I used to ask to have it
played again and again ..... and I'd prance around the
room with one arm in the air imagining I was a great
dancer. ..... I really don't know where I got the idea
but I used to do it almost every day for ages.
It was as if ..... the music and my brain ..... worked
together.
(PAUSE.) The strange thing is ..... I don't think it's like
that for Sarah. We've never talked about it ..... but I
just have that feeling. I watched her dance in last
year's show ..... looked into her eyes and there was
nothing there ..... nothing.

LEANING AGAINST THE CHAIR

They knew I was upset when I couldn't go dancing,
so mum said "You can go to speech and drama
classes." That's why I do drama. So here I am .....
and I quite like it, especially when we make up plays
of our own ..... makes you think about all sorts of
things.
(PAUSING TO SMILE.) They said classes would give
me confidence.

MOVING AND SUDDENLY EXCLAIMING

Confidence! I'm absolutely terrified! ....
But there are some really good things ..... for a start it
doesn't matter what shape or size you are ..... and our
teacher is excellent ..... treats us all like individuals .....
(PAUSING THOUGHTFULLY.) ..... with respect. ..... We
spend a lot of time just talking. It's about the only
time that anyone actually listens to what I have to
say. ..... She always makes time for each one of us.

SITTING

The only real trouble is that we have to do so much work on our own ..... and this doesn't somehow seem quite natural. I sometimes have to do a speech with just one person sitting listening. Well, you wouldn't get that in a real theatre, would you? Just one person? ..... at least, I'd hope not.
(PAUSE.) The **real** reason that I wanted to dance is that dancers get lots more chances to appear on stage in shows ..... and it is far far easier to work together in a class.
(PAUSE.) On the other hand, dance is rather .....
(GROPING FOR THE WORD.) ..... negative. They're always talking about 'corrections'. I hear them after class,
"What corrections did she give you?" .....
As if you must get something wrong if you are ever going to learn. Yes, I know that's true sometimes ..... but not **all** the time. I even overheard one girl say about a visiting teacher,
"She gave us brilliant corrections!"

MOVING

I'm probably better off sticking to speech and drama, even if I do have to do so much on my own. After all, we're all on our own, in a way, aren't we? You are. I am. **Everyone** is. We **all** are.
(PAUSE.) Sometimes, I feel nobody entirely understands me ..... and I'm glad!
(PAUSE.) I often dance for myself ..... but only when nobody's looking.

STANDING STILL

I shall never forget first hearing 'Swan Lake'.

EXIT.

ACTING NOTES

As with all the best acting this needs to be very simple, very direct, thoughtful and sincere. Try to focus attention on how Alison felt about not being allowed to attend dancing classes and imagine the sense of hurt she experienced at watching her sister. This speech will only 'work' if your listener follows your thought-line and the pauses are there to enable you to 'think aloud'. However, it is not entirely depressing because Alison has a good sense of humour and enjoys the world of imagination. Don't move for the sake of it and don't be afraid of stillness in this speech; on the other hand remember how strong 'body language' can be in revealing mood. The language of the speech is deliberately conversational and you should use your own regional accent without inhibition, whatever it is.

EVACUEE

During the Second World War all the schoolchildren from the Port of Dover were evacuated to rural Wales. For most of these children this was the first time that they had been away from their parents and although usually received with great kindness many were very homesick. This speech is based on an interview with an elderly gentleman who remembers being evacuated.

THE STAGE REPRESENTS A SMALL SPARSELY FURNISHED BEDROOM WITH A WINDOW LOOKING OUT AT THE 'BLACK MOUNTAINS'.

ALAN: *LOOKING OUT OF THE WINDOW*

> They call those the 'Black' mountains. Mrs Owen said that they aren't really black when you get up close to them but the sun never shines on them directly so they always look black.
> *(PAUSE.)* I've never seen mountains before. This place feels like the end of the earth. That's what m' Auntie Jessie said,
> "Going away to the ends of the earth!"
> It certainly felt like it on that train. It bumped along for hours and hours. I thought we never would get here.

> *MOVING TO A CHAIR*

> Back in Dover, when all the other kids were standing around me on the platform, it looked ...... it looked as if the whole town was there at the station. Kids were crying, my mum was crying, my sister was crying. I didn't cry. I wanted to ..... but I couldn't. I just felt numb ..... sort of dead inside. I was too scared to cry.

> *GOING TO A SMALL BAG OR CASE*

> We couldn't bring much with us ..... but I did bring this notebook ..... I keep it hidden in here so that my sister can't read it. She has to share this room. I'm glad, but she's very noisy sometimes. I say to her
> "Don't you ever stop talking?"
> She just laughs when I say that. ..... They let me bring this model ambulance. My dad made it for me and it reminds me of home.

> *LOOKING AT THE MODEL THOUGHTFULLY*

42

I've never been away from home before, neither has my sister. I didn't know what to expect. Mr and Mrs Owen are very nice but I think they are a bit old fashioned. At home we get hot water from a tap in the bathroom or kitchen if m' Dad lights the boiler. But here, Mrs Owen brings us hot water in a jug and we get washed by that 'washstand' over there. I'd never seen one of those before! I don't mind too much; I don't wash much anyway ..... I have what m' mum calls 'a lick'.

MOVING ACROSS THE ROOM

I like it when Mr Owen takes me on the farm. At first all the village kids used to stare at me but now they say 'hello' and I'll probably get to know them. Mrs Owen milks the cows and she let me have a go!

SHUDDERING AS HE RECALLS

It was peculiar! I didn't know it was like **that!** Fancy having to do that every day.
(PAUSE) We **did** go into the countryside around Dover sometimes but we never really saw the people working with the animals. Before the war dad worked in the docks, helping with the ferries, so we didn't know any farmers.
(SIGHING.) There's a lot of things I'm having to get used to here.

SITTING

I just wish my sister wasn't so unhappy. She's so homesick and I promised I'd try to keep her cheerful.

SHIFTING HIS POSITION

But it's not easy. If you're homesick you're homesick, there's not much I can do about it. Sometimes she seems quite all right and then, without any warning, starts crying and says she wants to go home. Well, we **can't** go home. We've just gotta stay here until the war is over. I didn't ask to come here, it's not my fault.

(GETTING RATHER INDIGNANT.)
I keep telling her it's not my fault. What am I
supposed to do? I'm probably more unhappy than
she is at the end of the day!

LOOKING OUT OF THE WINDOW AGAIN

But at this time of day it's difficult to be **too** unhappy,
when you can see the sun ..... and follow as it
gradually disappears behind those mountains. I
always come up here to watch. See that? Now! as
it sinks down. ..... There, that .....

MAKING A SHAPE WITH HIS HANDS

..... almost square black shape with the sharp edge .....
for a moment ..... the sun ..... glows around that shape
like a fire ..... and then vanishes. ..... There, its gone.

WATCHING INTENTLY

That's wonderful. I'd love to go to that place where
the sun touches the mountain top.
(PAUSING THOUGHTFULLY.) All there is to see is an
outline of the mountain. so I'm sure nobody could live
there. ..... I try to get my sister to watch with me but
she won't stay still long enough. I sometimes
wonder if anyone else watches. ..... It's difficult to
imagine that there's a war going on. It doesn't make
sense. When you see something like that, you
wonder why people want to fight!
(PAUSE.) Perhaps I really am the only sensible
person left on earth.

*MOVING THOUGHTFULLY AFTER A VERY LONG
PAUSE*

(CALLING.) Mrs Owen. Would you like me
to help you?

EXIT.

ACTING NOTES

If you do not know anything about the way in which people lived during the Second World War it is important to find out before starting to prepare this speech.. The piece is actually based on a school project where pupils interviewed elderly people about their memories of the war and the importance of this kind of 'research' must not be overlooked or underestimated. You must try to imagine what it would be like to be sent away from your home to live with another family at a time when there was far less travel than there is today. The most important feature of this speech is the focus on the mountains: you must see these in your imagination and convey that to your listener. Concentrate also on simple detail like the notebook and the model and try to convey concern over your sister's unhappiness.

The evacuee may be played by a performer of either sex.

PINNOCHIO

This scene is from a dramatised version of the famous children's story. Pinnochio is a wooden puppet made by the wood carver, Geppetto and he has come to life. Geppetto has attempted to teach him good behaviour and has arranged for him to attend school. Pinnochio is walking home.

THE STAGE IS ALMOST BARE AND DIFFERENT AREAS REPRESENT DIFFERENT LOCATIONS. THERE IS A PAINTED SIGN WHICH READS 'MARIONETTE THEATRE' WITH A PICTURE OF PUPPETS DANCING.

PINNOCHIO: *TURNS AND ADDRESSES THE AUDIENCE*

I'll be in trouble when I get home, I know it! But oh! It was such fun when I found I could run like all the other children! I ran like a racehorse! I jumped like a rabbit! And my poor father, Geppetto, chased after me, shouting
"Catch him! Catch him!"
but when the people saw he was chasing a wooden puppet, all they did was stare in amazement, then laugh until their sides nearly burst.

HE REACHES GEPPETTO'S HOUSE

Here I am, home at last. Father. I'm back! Don't be cross with me! I'll be good from now on. Father?

HE ENTERS THE HOUSE AND LOOKS AROUND BUT NOBODY IS ABOUT. HE TAKES OUT AN ABC BOOK

(LOOKING AT HIS BOOK UNCERTAINLY.) A .... Aaaye! B ..... B ..... Beeeye! Keeye?

HE GIVES UP, SNAPS THE BOOK SHUT AND LOOKS UP AT THE AUDIENCE

At school today I will learn to read immediately. Tomorrow I will learn to write, and the day after tomorrow I will learn all about maths so I can do enormous sums in my head. Like three billion, two hundred million and seventy-six multiplied by ..... by ..... twenty-nine decasquillion equals .... equals? .... Well! I'll be able to do it the day after tomorrow. Then I will know so much that I can earn heaps of money. And with the very first pennies I earn I will buy my father a nice new cloth coat. But why do I say cloth? It shall be all of gold and silver with diamond buttons. That poor man really deserves it, for in order that I may go to school he sold his coat to buy me a book ..... in this cold weather! Only a loving father would do so much for his son! Oh well, off to school!

HE STARTS WALKING AS MUSIC BEGINS TO PLAY IN THE BACKGROUND AND HE STOPS TO LISTEN

That's a nice tune! No, I must go to school. I mustn't be late on my first day!

HE STARTS TO WALK AGAIN BUT THE MUSIC GROWS LOUDER AND SEEMS TO PHYSICALLY HOLD HIM BACK

I wonder what's going on?

HE SEES A PAINTED SIGN

Puppets? A puppet show?! It's a real puppet show! With puppets just like me! I wonder if they will know that I'm a puppet? That I am like them? ..... Perhaps I'll just stay for a minute and watch.

PINNOCHIO DISAPPEARS INSIDE THE THEATRE

ACTING NOTES

Ideally you should provide yourself with a battery operated cassette or CD player for this scene and unobtrusively start playing music before the second section of the speech. Initially you will need to work on the way in which a wooden jointed puppet would move and then convey the idea that Pinnochio is extremely easily distracted and very mischievous. Be absolutely clear in your mind as to where the different locations are and take trouble to represent them using a few chairs set at angles which will define areas whilst enabling your audience to watch your facial expressions.

N.B.   The performer should provide recorded music if possible.

from the play PINNOCHIO by Claudia Leaf
first performed by the Channel Theatre Company
used with permission

HIGH STAKES

This speech is taken from a play presented to secondary schools by one of Britain's leading theatre in education companies. It explores the problems of gambling which often start very early in life.

THE ACTING SPACE IS EMPTY EXCEPT FOR A CHAIR. STEVE ENTERS AND TALKS DIRECTLY TO THE AUDIENCE.

STEVE: I don't know when I first went into one of those places ..... but I do remember the very first time I had a go. It was when we were on holiday by the seaside ..... I was only about nine or ten.

MOVING TO ANOTHER PLACE AND RECREATING THE SENSE OF EXCITEMENT WITH VOICE AND MOVEMENT

Now an arcade is a brilliant place! Flashing lights, colour, noise! The beep of the machines, the jingles and of course the superb sound of the pay out! I remember I clutched hold of my fifty pence piece. What to spend it on? The change machine turned it into 10p's and I was ready! Some of the machines seemed too complicated but I thought, "One day **I'll** be able to play them!" I put my first 10p in. Five goes. I pushed the play button. The reels went round ..... an orange, a cherry and a joker. I pressed again ..... an apple and two jokers. The nudge button flashed and beeped! I felt my heart beating faster and faster. What shall I do? I had to make up my mind! I held the jokers ..... round and round the reels spun. Please! Please! .... Lights! Music! Coins! Everybody looking at me! Three jokers. Four quid! I'd won the jackpot! Even Katie was impressed. After that I went to the arcade every day. ..... And when we got home I found out there weren't just arcades at the seaside.

CHANGE OF PLACE AND PACE

'Cos the truth was the money I won went to buy the presents from the machines down the snooker club! And did they have a **really** smart machine there! The whole thing erupted ..... bright lights, loud jingles and fifty quid!

(PAUSE.) When you win everybody's your friend. You feel fantastic, you feel great! ..... but sometimes I couldn't always get enough money to play ..... so that's when I did a bit of shoplifting. ..... I didn't want to ..... you know how it is. When I got caught and the police brought me home mum and dad weren't too impressed.

SITTING AND REMEMBERING FONDLY

I really fancied Julia so we all made arrangements to meet the next night down the White Horse. I was a bit worried she might not like me when she saw me again. Her and Mel were fatal.
(PAUSE.) So I started playing the machine. By the time they arrived It was about ready to pay out. I didn't want some jerk winning the jackpot ..... but of course, when they came, I had to be sociable.

WALKING TO ANOTHER POINT

(LONG PAUSE.) That cheque book came in really handy. The bloke it belonged to must have been away 'cos I went on using it for a couple of weeks without anyone finding out. Every day I went down the snooker club to play the machines ..... Easy! They cashed my cheques even though they knew me as Steve and the name on the cheques was John Bridges! It was crazy! I even started believing I was him. I wish I was. I must have pumped a fortune into that machine! Every day I stood in front of it. Me ..... alone against the odds. Time didn't matter. It was a battle. I had to beat it! And I did. ..... The trouble was I never know when to stop and it all went back in again.

SITTING AND COMPLETELY CHANGING THE MOOD

You can bet on anything when you're banged up on remand. In there we used to bet on what rain drop would run down the window first.
(LONG PAUSE.) Afterward, down the arcade ..... when I talked to older blokes who've been gambling all their lives ..... I realised what could happen to me.
(PAUSE.) They tell me you're never cured ..... but I just know I can stop.

*CLENCHING HIS HANDS IN A DETERMINED GESTURE AND PAUSING
BEFORE MOVING OFF*

EXIT.

ACTING NOTES

It is astonishing how many young people become addicted to gambling and you need
to try to understand what Steve is saying here before you begin to work on the speech.
He takes us through his gradual descent into near disaster and he tries to present a
'cool' image of his behaviour. You need to work hard to convince your audience that
what has happened was almost inevitable and yet must acknowledge that, at any point,
Steve need not have continued. Imagine an audience gathered round you and treat
them as if they have come to hear you explain yourself. Make the acting style simple
and strong and be sure to make the transition between the initial air of bravado and the
gradual painful realisation and awareness.

This scene could be played by a female with minor changes to the text.

HIGH STAKES by Philip Dart
first presented by the Channel Theatre Company
used with permission

50

OLIVER TWIST

Oliver, a poor orphan, has been taken away from the workhouse where he grew up to be apprenticed to an undertaker. The undertaker's wife, Mrs. Sowerberry, has just shown him where he is to sleep at night.

OLIVER IS LEFT ALONE HOLDING A LAMP IN THE GLOOMY UNDERTAKER'S SHOP. THERE IS A BENCH OR SURFACE CENTRE STAGE REPRESENTING A COUNTER AND WE ARE ASKED TO IMAGINE PLANKS OF TIMBER AND HALF-MADE COFFINS LYING AROUND.

OLIVER: She said I had to sleep here under the counter.
..... Oh! it's so dark in here. ..... I suppose she meant under there?

HE MOVES TOWARDS THE COUNTER

(IMITATING HER.) "Your bed's under the counter," she said,
"you don't mind sleeping among the coffins,
I suppose? But it doesn't much matter whether you do or don't, 'cos you can't sleep anywhere else!"
Well thank you, Mrs Sowerberry ..... that's very kind of you. This is terrible, this place is terrible.

PUTTING DOWN THE LAMP

It's so full of shadows ...... they make me freeze. .....
Look at that! ..... a coffin. ..... I can't stop trembling .....
I know there are ghosts here.

MOVING AWAY FROM THE COFFIN

Any moment now a body is going to rise up out of that coffin ..... any moment now. ..... I can't look.

CURLING UP SMALL

This is where they make them ..... the coffins ..... and I've got to stay here ..... all day and all night.

PEERING AT A LONG ROW OF COFFIN LIDS

Those planks of wood over there ..... all the same shape ..... the same pale colour. They look like ghosts with high shoulders ..... waiting for me!

51

...... And all these snippets of black cloth on the floor. ..... All black, everything black.

LOOKING AT A PICTURE ON THE WALL

And this is what it's all for. Look at those silent men in stiff collars and that ..... that carriage drawn by black horses with black plumes.
(LONG PAUSE.) It's so very hot in here ...... stuffy .....
suffocating. *(TAKING A BREATH.)* That smell ..... wood smell ..... is suffocating.

SITTING

And now I'm all alone again. I'm all alone ..... I don't miss anyone. There's nobody I want to be with .....
and yet ..... I'm so lonely and scared and I wish .....
I wish I could be in **my** grave.

STARTING AND TREMBLING

No, no. I can't look. ...... Over there ..... rising out of the coffin. ..... It's coming for me. It's coming for me.

TRYING TO HIDE FROM AN IMAGINED GHOST AND LOOKING OUT THROUGH HIS FINGERS

Don't be afraid, Oliver. There's nothing there.
(LONG PAUSE.) I only wish I had a friend, just one friend, to care for or to care about me ...... but I haven't so I'd best forget about it and get into bed.

LOOKING UNDER THE COUNTER

So this is my narrow bed. I think it would be better if this could be my coffin.

CRAWLING UNDER THE COUNTER AND SETTLING DOWN

Then I could be calm and there would be tall grass waving over my head and the sound of an old bell to send me to sleep.

HE SLEEPS

Oliver needs to be ragged and barefoot for this speech. You will benefit from a few props and something which gives a sense of your being able to crawl underneath it. Give careful thought to your entry into this dark space and take time to make your reactions to the shadows and other frightening objects around the room. The effect of such gloom is to make Oliver feel timid, afraid and utterly alone: work on this idea before you even move around the space. Try to feel small and overwhelmed by the situation. Oliver is talking with himself here so try to create that idea of 'inner dialogue' and let your audience 'read' your thoughts through your eyes and facial expression. Find out something about the working conditions of children in the nineteenth century before attempting this scene and be sure to read Oliver Twist!

from ALONE IN THE NINETEENTH CENTURY by Ken Pickering
a dramatisation of the novel Oliver Twist by Charles Dickens

A LADY GOES TO WAR

This is the opening speech from a play presented to middle school students by the Channel Theatre Company. The scene takes place in Haskell's Hall of Fame and a school party is visiting the museum.

THE STAGE REPRESENTS A SMALL GALLERY. TWO CHAIRS CAN BE USED FOR EXHIBITS AND THERE ARE TWO DUST SHEETS TO HAND.

THE CURATOR: *ENTERS*

And here we come to the last, and one of my favourite, exhibits in my 'Great Women in History' series. Yes, as you can see, it is the 'Lady with the Lamp', Florence Nightingale. Now, I'm sure you are familiar with the story of this amazing lady who became a nurse and went to help the poor soldiers during the Crimean war some hundred and fifty years ago. Here, she is depicted on her famous rounds at the Barrack Hospital at Scutari. Please note the lamp. This is a genuine Turkish lamp which I had great difficulty in obtaining. Sometimes Florence is portrayed with the wrong kind of lamp; sometimes the lamp looks more suited to Aladdin than the founder of modern nursing. However, we here at Haskell's Hall of Fame, endeavour to make every effort to be authentic. We may not have the money or resources of the larger museums but we place a high price on authenticity. Now, where was I? Oh, yes. With lamp in hand this kind, gentle, soft hearted woman visited the beds of the sick and dying men to offer comfort. As you can see, here she is offering comfort to a poor wounded soldier. The soldiers considered her a saint and, of course, her legend lives on today. I think Florence is appropriate as our final exhibit, don't you?
(PAUSE.) That concludes our little tour of the Hall of Fame today. Thank you all very much for being such an attentive audience. I hope you have had an enjoyable time. There is a small plate at the door for any gratuities you may wish to leave.
(POINTEDLY.) Tips to those who are unaware of the Latin.

A PUPIL RAISES A HAND OR SHOUTS OUT

Yes?

*RATHER IRRITATED THAT THE QUESTION IS ABOUT
THE WHEREABOUTS OF THE TOILET*

Down there on the right.
(CALLING AFTER THE PUPIL)
But please be quick as I am about to lock up.

*THE SCHOOL PARTY MAKES FOR THE EXIT
HURRIEDLY LEAVING THE CURATOR ALONE*

I don't know. I'm in a rush to get home and they
have to wait till the last minute to go to the toilet.
I hate school parties anyway. You have to let them
in for half the price, they never listen, they make a
mess and never tip. Right, Florence, it's about time
you were put to bed.

COVERING HER UP

And you George, you poor old wounded soldier.

COVERING HIM UP

Now, the lights.

*DUCKING BEHIND TO SWITCH OFF THE DISPLAY
LIGHTS*

Better do the same for Boadicea, Liz the First and
Queen Vic and then I'll be off home.

MOVING OFF

Chewing gum! You wouldn't believe it, only the
other day I found chewing gum stuck to Queen
Victoria's crown. Some people have no respect!

EXIT.

ACTING NOTES

You must be passionate about the exhibits and always disappointed when that
enthusiasm is not shared. Imagine your audience standing near you on the stage area
and work hard to keep their attention. The curator is confident and firm footed but will
move and point to things very busily. There will need to be moments of great stillness
as well as various shifts of focus. Remember that the curator is used to public speaking
and that there is nothing intimate about the way in which the visiting parties are
addressed.

The curator may be played by a performer of either sex

from the play NIGHTINGALE - A LADY GOES TO WAR by Philip Dart
first performed by the Channel Theatre Company
used with permission

SIR GAWAIN AND THE GREEN KNIGHT

This is the opening speech from Sir Gawain and the Green Knight, an adaptation of the wonderful medieval poem telling a story of adventure and daring at the court of King Arthur.

THE BARE STAGE REPRESENTS AN OPEN AIR AREA IMMEDIATELY OUTSIDE KING ARTHUR'S COURT. THE YOUNG MINSTREL SPEAKS DIRECTLY TO THE AUDIENCE.

MINSTREL: *LOOKING STRAIGHT AT THE AUDIENCE*

Welcome to Camelot! To the court of King Arthur and his beautiful Queen Guinevere.
(RATHER INTIMATELY.) I shouldn't really be out here talking to you .....
but I'm so exhausted I really had to take a break.
(BREATHES DEEPLY.) You see, we've been celebrating Christmas and for **fifteen** days there has been singing and dancing and feasting. I just don't know where they **put** all that food. .....
It makes me feel like an inflated pig's bladder to think of it.
(SIGHING.) It's no good, I shall have to sit down.

SITS

Now, you see, because I'm a musician, ...
yes, I know, I am very young but you will have to believe me, I do have a beautiful voice
and I can play several instruments ......
so **I** have to organise all the music, and I tell you, they are **never** satisfied.

STANDS AND MOVES OVER TO ADDRESS CLOSE MEMBERS OF THE AUDIENCE

All the gallant Knights are here ..... Sir Lancelot, Sir Bedevere, Sir Gawain ...... he's a remarkable man, you know! And, of course, all their fair ladies.
(SIGHING.) And the revelry just seems to go on and on.

MOVING

The trouble is, I think King Arthur is actually rather bored with all this feasting. I get the feeling that he would much sooner be off on some adventure or having someone tell him an exciting story. I've done my best ..... I've sung them so many songs.

(SIGHING.) Then, when I can't think of a new one, I just hope that they have drunk too much to notice that I'm singing one that I sang a few hours earlier. I'm sure some of the ladies notice but they're too nice to say so.

(PAUSING.)

At least, some of them are!

(ALMOST WHISPERING.) So, with all that going on in there, I've just slipped out here into the frosty air for a moment.

(SNIFFING.) Oh, it smells sweet ..... the wood smoke. There's a great log fire crackling in there ..... and when they roast the meat on it ..... it ..... it makes you feel so **hungry**. And, do you know, they often forget to give me anything!

"Come on, sing us another song!" they shout. But I'm absolutely starving ..... it's not fair. I think that they should feed their Minstrel **before** they feed their dogs ..... but not a bit of it ...... those huge hounds get all the best bits and, if I'm lucky, I get a few scraps.

(SHRUGGING AND CHANGING MOOD.)

Well, as you will have gathered, I like a good moan. I suppose I'm very fortunate, really, to be working at the court of the great King Arthur at my age.

(VERY DIRECT.) I have a strange feeling that something odd is going to happen very soon. Although there is all this celebration, there is a rather gloomy atmosphere in there ...... as if we are waiting for something unusual to arrive.

LOOKING AROUND

It all seems very **still,** and although everyone still seems to want to sing, everything keeps going very quiet.

(PAUSING.) I'm not sure what to make of it.

(SUDDENLY CHANGING MOOD.) But I tell you one thing. If King Arthur catches me out here talking to you like this I'll be in terrible trouble. ......

TURNING TO LOOK BEHIND

I'm afraid it's too late ..... here he comes.

RUNNING OFF

Yes, your Majesty.

EXIT.

ACTING NOTES

The Minstrel needs to be a very lively and light-footed character and the effectiveness of the scene comes from the chatty address to the audience. Remember that the Minstrel has just 'popped out' from court duties and there is always the possibility that the king will be calling for more music and wondering where his minstrel has gone. Use the open space of the stage to give the impression of the wide outdoors at night and imagine the sounds of revelry and the smell of wood smoke as you speak. Try to take the audience into your confidence as if you are telling them a secret and enjoy the slight exaggeration of your description of the feasting and hunger.

The minstrel may be played by a performer of either sex.

from the poem SIR GAWAIN AND THE GREEN KNIGHT
adapted for the stage by Michael Herzog and Ken Pickering
published by J. Garnet Miller Ltd
used with permission

JANE EYRE

This is a dramatised version of the great nineteenth-century novel by Charlotte Bronte. In this scene Jane tells how she started the period of her life at Lowood School which provided such a harsh existence that some girls did not survive.

THERE IS A SINGLE CHAIR ON STAGE. JANE SPEAKS ALMOST INTIMATELY ABOUT EVENTS AND USES THE VOICES OF THE HOUSEKEEPER AND HELEN AS SHE RECALLS THEM.

JANE: *SPEAKING DIRECTLY TO THE AUDIENCE*

I remember but little of the journey: I only know that the day seemed to me of a preternatural length, and that we appeared to travel over hundreds of miles of road until we arrived at Lowood School. After I had waited a while in the entrance hall the housekeeper appeared and addressed me:

(HOUSEKEEPER:) "Is there a little girl called Jane Eyre here?"

"Yes, Miss."

(HOUSEKEEPER:) "Are you alone?"

"Yes, Miss."

(HOUSEKEEPER:) " Well, you'd better be put straight to bed."

MOVING TO ANOTHER PART OF THE STAGE, REACTING AS SHE REMEMBERS THE BITTER COLD AND THE UNPLEASANT EXPERIENCES.

The night passed rapidly: I was too tired even to dream. I awoke to a loud bell ringing. Day had not yet begun to dawn, but the other girls were up and dressing. I too rose reluctantly; it was bitter cold, and I dressed as well as I could for shivering, and washed when there was a basin at liberty. Again the bell rung: all formed in file, two and two, and in that order descended the stairs and entered the cold and dimly lit schoolroom. Here prayers were read out, the day's collect was repeated, then certain texts of scripture were said, and to these succeeded a protracted reading of chapters in the Bible, which lasted an hour. The bell now sounded again and we marched

into another room to breakfast. How glad I was to behold a prospect of getting something to eat! I devoured a spoonful or two of my portion without thinking of its taste; but the first edge of hunger blunted, I perceived I had got in hand a nauseous mess. Breakfast was over and none had breakfasted. Thanks being returned for what we had not got, and a second hymn chanted and the refectory was evacuated for the school room. The teachers then gave lessons in geography, history, grammar, writing and arithmetic. Each lesson lasted an hour, measured by the clock, which at last struck twelve. At that time one of our teachers suddenly ordered that we were to have extra rations of bread and cheese; and the bread and cheese was presently brought in and distributed. Then the order was given 'to the garden' and I saw a girl sitting on a stone bench nearby reading a book.
(PAUSE.) This is how I recollect our conversation.

SITTING AND ACTING OUT HER MEMORY OF EVENTS

"Is your book interesting?"

(HELEN:)   "I like it."

"What is it about?"

(HELEN:)   *(OFFERING THE BOOK.)* "You may look at it."

"Thank you. Does that lady who said we were to have some bread and cheese own this school?"

(HELEN:)   "Miss Temple? Oh no! I wish she did. She is the Superintendent: she has to answer to Mr Brocklehurst for all she does."

"Does he live here?"

(HELEN:)   "No - two miles off, at a large hall."

"Is he a good man?"

(HELEN:)   "He is a clergyman, and is said to do a great deal of good."

"Did you say that lady was called Miss Temple?"

(HELEN:) "Yes."

"And what are the other teachers called?"

(HELEN:) "The one with red cheeks is called Miss Smith; she attends to the work, and cuts out - for we make our own clothes, our frocks and pelisses, and everything. The little one with black hair is Miss Scatcherd: she teaches history and grammar, and hears the second class repetitions, and the one who wears a shawl, and has a pocket handkerchief tied to her side with a yellow ribband, is Madame Pierrot: she comes from Lisle, in France, and teaches French."

"Do you like the teachers?"

(HELEN:) "Well enough."

"Do you like the small dark one, and the Madame? I cannot pronounce her name as you do."

(HELEN:) "Miss Scatcherd is hasty - you must take care not to offend her. Madame Pierrot is not a bad sort of person."

"But Miss Temple is the best, isn't she?"

(HELEN:) "Miss Temple is very good, and very clever."

"Have you been here long?"

(HELEN:) "Two years."

"Are you an orphan?"

(HELEN:) "My mother is dead."

"Are you happy here?"

(HELEN:) "You ask rather too many questions. I have given you answers enough for the present; now I want to read."

STANDING

62

Such was my first meeting with Helen Burns .....
a meeting which I shall never forget.

EXIT.

ACTING NOTES

This scene presents a real but exciting challenge. Don't be put off by the vocabulary or the rather quaint descriptions, this novel has continued to fascinate generations of readers of all ages. Scenes in which the performer has to both 'tell' and 'show' are familiar in the modern theatre. At times you can give physical indications of what is happening in your memory but do not attempt to reproduce every detail except through your voice and body language. When it comes to the imagined 'duologues' with the Housekeeper and Helen convey the sense of conversation with slight shifts in the angle of your head and the pitch of your voice together with the registration of every emotion and thought in your face and eyes. The names of these characters are indicated in brackets to show how the dialogue works and you must make a clear distinction between conversation sections and the direct address to the audience. Remember that Jane was living at a time when 'ladylike' behaviour would have been drummed into her so wear a long skirt and a tightly belted waist to help with characterisation and movement. Give plenty of thought to your footwear, too.

JANE EYRE adapted for the stage by Philip Dart and Ken Pickering
first performed by the Channel Theatre Company
used with permission

THE IMMORTAL HARVEY

This is the opening speech from The Immortal Harvey, set in Padua in 1602. William Harvey is a young medical student at Padua University. He went on to become the first person to discover the blood circulation system.

THERE IS A DESK OR TABLE PILED WITH LARGE BOOKS AND A COUPLE OF CHAIRS TO ONE SIDE OF THE ACTING AREA AND WE ARE ASKED TO IMAGINE SOME SCREENS ON WHICH ARE LARGE ANATOMICAL DRAWINGS. HARVEY IS STANDING AS IF LOOKING DOWN FROM A HIGH GALLERY. HE SPEAKS QUIETLY TO THE AUDIENCE AS IF HE IS AWARE OF A PERFORMANCE IN PROGRESS.

HARVEY: *MOVING NEARER THE AUDIENCE*

This theatre is a curious place. From this upper gallery you can clearly see all the action. In fact, although there are five of these concentric galleries I am still only about twenty-five feet away from the focus of our attention.
(PAUSE.) I love this place ..... the oak panelling ..... the light from the candelabra. There is nowhere quite like it ..... nearly two hundred and fifty people can watch. ..... It's like looking down into a funnel to the stone pit at the bottom. And there, Fabricius, our great teacher dissects human and animal corpses to instruct us in anatomy.

MOVING AWAY FROM THE GALLERY EDGE

He designed this theatre for that purpose. I don't think Fabricius actually enjoys teaching. He gets very irritated by the rowdy behaviour of students ...... particularly the Germans and it doesn't take much for him to cancel or shorten a course. But there's no doubt that he's established this University of Padua as one of the great centres for the study of physik ..... "Go to Padua" they told me when I was finishing at Cambridge ..... and "When Fabricius is interested he's brilliant."

LOOKING AROUND AS IF THE STUDENTS WERE PRESENT

One of the problems is that he delights in dissecting all kinds of animals. He teaches, as it were, comparative anatomy but of course the duller students can't see the relevance of it. They argue that they are just here to study human anatomy. ..... It's so typical of the small-minded attitude of so many students ..... If it doesn't precisely help them to pass an examination they are not interested. ..... How do they think we advance the frontiers of medicine without experiment and careful observation of **all** life? *(PAUSE.)* The trouble is, this university is virtually run by the students. It's not at all like Cambridge. Here, the students elect their teachers and then each national group elects a consiliaris to represent them on the governing council. ..... The English students elected me. It's a very difficult job. There's a lot of violence between the different racial groups. ...... These days .....

DRAWING A DAGGER

...... I tend to draw this first and talk afterwards. *(LONG PAUSE.)* I sometimes long for the predictable order of Folkestone; even for the chill of school dormitories in Canterbury ....

HE MOVES TO ANOTHER PART OF THE STAGE AND SITS AT THE TABLE PERUSING LARGE BOOKS

ACTING NOTES

You <u>must</u> understand the exact shape of the 'theatre' you are describing before you prepare this scene and you can enjoy the small joke which you play on the audience by leaving them a little uncertain at first as to what sort of theatre you are talking about. Harvey must convey his tremendous feeling of excitement and of slight irritation here: he is personally on the verge of one of the most important discoveries in the entire history of medicine and he acts as guide to the audience in explaining to them what is going on. Use a great deal of variation of pace in this speech and use pauses to introduce new ideas. There is a large change of mood in the final few lines and you will need to slacken the pace in order to make the end 'fade'. Don't be put off by the ancient expression 'physik' which simply means 'medicine' or the pronunciation of Fabricius

(Fa-breek i us). Remember that, in the early seventeenth century, people went to university as young teenagers and that it was quite usual for students of all nationalities to mix because most of the teaching was in Latin!

from the play THE IMMORTAL HARVEY by Ken Pickering
first performed by the Images Theatre Company
at the Operating Theatre Museum, London and the Penny Theatre, Canterbury

ADDITIONAL TITLES

All books may be ordered direct from:
DRAMATIC LINES   PO BOX 201   TWICKENHAM   TW2 5RQ
tel: 020 8296 9502   fax: 020 8296 9503

MONOLOGUES

THE SIEVE AND OTHER SCENES
Heather Stephens
ISBN 0 9522224 0 X

The Sieve contains unusual short original monologues valid for junior acting examinations. The material in The Sieve has proved popular with winning entries worldwide in drama festival competitions. Although these monologues were originally written for the 8-14 year age range they have been used by adult actors for audition and performance pieces. Each monologue is seen through the eyes of a young person with varied subject matter including tough social issues such as fear, 'Television Spinechiller', senile dementia, 'Seen Through a Glass Darkly' and withdrawal from the world in 'The Sieve'. Other pieces include: 'A Game of Chicken', 'The Present', 'Balloon Race' and a widely used new adaptation of Hans Christian Andersen's 'The Little Match Girl' in monologue form.

CABBAGE AND OTHER SCENES
Heather Stephens
ISBN 0 9522224 5 0

Following the success of The Sieve, Heather Stephens has written an additional book of monologues with thought provoking and layered subject matter valid for junior acting examinations. The Cabbage monologues were originally written for the 8-14 year age range but have been used by adult actors for audition and performance pieces. The Aberfan slag heap disaster issues are graphically confronted in 'Aberfan Prophecy' and 'The Surviving Twin' whilst humorous perceptions of life are observed by young people in 'The Tap Dancer' and 'Cabbage'. Other pieces include: 'The Dinner Party Guest', 'Nine Lives' and a new adaptation of Robert Browning's 'The Pied Piper' seen through the eyes of the crippled child.

DUOLOGUES

PEARS
Heather Stephens
ISBN 0 9522224 6 9

Heather Stephens has written layered, thought provoking and unusual short original duologues to provide new material for speech and drama festival candidates in the 8-14 year age range. The scenes have also been widely used for junior acting examinations and in a variety of school situations and theatrical applications. Challenging topics in Pears include the emotive issues of child migration, 'Blondie', 'The Outback Institution' and bullying 'Bullies', other scenes examine friendship, 'The Best of Friends', 'The Row' and envy, 'Never the Bridesmaid'. New duologue adaptations of part scenes from the classic play, 'Peace' by Aristophanes and 'Oliver Twist' by Charles Dickens are also included.

SCENES

JELLY BEANS
Joseph McNair Stover
ISBN 0 9522224 7 7

The distinctive style and deceptively simple logic of American writer Joseph McNair Stover has universal appeal with scenes that vary in tone from whimsical to serious and focus on young peoples relationships in the contemporary world. The collection of 10-15 minute original scenes for 2, 3 and 4 players is suitable for 11 year olds through to adult. Minimal use of sets and props makes pieces ideal for group acting examinations, classroom drama, assemblies and various other theatrical applications and have been used with success at Young Writers Workshops to teach the elements of scriptwriting and dramatic development.

LESSONS

DRAMA LESSONS IN ACTION
Antoinette Line
ISBN 0 9522224 2 6

Resource material suitable for classroom and assembly use, with lessons taught through improvisation for teachers of junior and secondary age pupils. These are not presented as 'model lessons' but provide ideas for adaptation and further development. The lessons include warm-up and speech exercises and themes are developed through feelings such as timidity, resentfulness, sensitivity and suspicion. The material can be used by groups of varying sizes and pupils are asked to respond to interesting texts from a diverse selection of well known authors including: Roald Dahl, Ogden Nash, Ted Hughes, Michael Rosen, and John Betjeman.

TEENAGE PLAYS

X-STACY
Margery Forde
ISBN 0 9522224 9 3

Margery Forde's powerful play centres on the rave culture and illicit teenage drug use and asks tough questions about family, friends and mutual responsibilities. The play has proved hugely successful in Australia and this English edition is published with extensive teachers' notes by Helen Radian, Lecturer of Drama at Queensland University of Technology, to enrich its value for the secondary school classroom, PSHE studies, English and drama departments.

WHAT IS THE MATTER WITH MARY JANE?
Wendy Harmer
ISBN 0 9522224 4 2

This monodrama about a recovering anorexic and bulimic takes the audience into the painful reality of a young woman afflicted by eating disorders. The play is based on the personal experience of actress Sancia Robinson and has proved hugely popular in Australia. It is written with warmth and extraordinary honesty and the language, humour and style appeal to current youth culture. A study guide for teachers and students by Dianne Mackenzie, Curriculum Officer for English and Drama, New South Wales is included in this English edition ensuring that the material is ideal for use in the secondary school classroom and for PSHE studies, drama departments in schools and colleges in addition to amateur and professional performance.

SHAKESPEARE THE REWRITES
Claire Jones
ISBN 0 9522224 8 5

A collection of short monologues and duologues for female players. The scenes are from rewrites of Shakespeare plays from 1670 to the present day written by authors seeking to embellish original texts for perfomances, to add prequels or sequels or to satisfy their own very personal ideas about production. This material is fresh and unusual and will provide exciting new audition and LAMDA examination material. Comparisons with the original Shakespeare text are fascinating and this book will provide a useful contribution to Theatre Study work from GCSE to beyond 'A' level. Contributors include James Thurber (Macbeth) Arnold Wesker (Merchant of Venice) and Peter Ustinov (Romanoff and Juliet). The collection also includes a most unusual Japanese version of Hamlet.

ONE ACT PLAYS

WILL SHAKESPEARE SAVE US!
WILL SHAKESPEARE SAVE THE KING!
Paul Nimmo
ISBN 0 9522224 1 8

Two versatile plays in which famous speeches and scenes from Shakespeare are acted out as part of a comic story about a bored king and his troupe of players.   These plays are suitable for the 11-18 year age range and have been produced with varying ages within the same cast and also performed by adults to a young audience. The plays can be produced as a double bill, alternatively each will stand on its own, performed by a minimum cast of 10 without a set, few props and modern dress or large cast, traditional set and costumes. The scripts are ideal for reading aloud by classes or groups and provide an excellent introduction to the works of Shakespeare. Both plays have been successfully performed on tour and at the Shakespeare's Globe in London.

SUGAR ON SUNDAYS AND OTHER PLAYS
Andrew Gordon
ISBN 0 9522224

A collection of six one act plays bringing history alive through drama. History is viewed through the eyes of ordinary people and each play is packed with details about everyday life, important events and developments of the period. The plays can be used as classroom drama, for school performances and group acting examinations and can also be used as shared texts for the literacy hour. The plays are suitable for children from Key Stage 2 upwards and are 40-50 minutes in length and explore Ancient Egypt, Ancient Greece, Anglo-Saxon and Viking Times, Victorian Britain and the Second World War.   A glossary of key words helps to develop children's historical understanding of National Curriculum History Topics and the plays provide opportunities for children to enjoy role play and performance.